THE
PYTHON BIBLE

VOLUME SIX

NEURAL NETWORKS

BY

FLORIAN DEDOV

TABLE OF CONTENT

INTRODUCTION

Machine learning is one of the most popular subjects of computer science at the moment. It is fascinating how computers are able to learn to solve complex problems, without specific instructions but just by looking at training data. With machine learning we made computers able to recognize and reproduce human voices, to recognize objects and to drive cars. Wherever big advances and achievements are made, we hear the term *deep learning*. Rarely do we hear that we made some radical progress with linear regression or with a basic classification algorithm. The technologies used are almost always neural networks.

Deep learning is a sub-field of machine learning, which is all about neural networks. These neural networks are inspired by the human brain and produce extraordinary results. They beat professional chess players, drive cars and outperform humans even in complex video games like Dota 2.

Furthermore, the speed of progress that we make in these fields makes it almost impossible to predict where all of this is going over the next couple of decades. But one thing is for sure: Those who understand machine learning and neural networks will have huge advantages over those, who will be overrun by these developments. Therefore, it makes a lot of sense to educate yourself on these subjects.

THIS BOOK

In this book, you will learn what neural networks are and how they work from scratch. You will also learn how to build and use them in the programming language Python. We will work with impressive examples and you will be astonished by some of the results.

What you will need for this book are advanced Python skills and a basic understanding of machine learning. Fundamental math skills are also beneficial. If you lack these skills, I recommend reading the previous volumes of this Python Bible Series, before proceeding. The first couple of volumes focus on the basic and intermediate concepts of Python. Then we learn some things about data science, machine learning and finance programming. This book is the sixth volume and a lot of knowledge from the previous volumes is required. However, you can also try to learn these skills from other sources. In this book though, there won't be any explanations of basic Python syntax or fundamental machine learning concepts.

Amazon Author Page: https://amzn.to/38D209r

HOW TO READ THIS BOOK

Fundamentally, it is your own choice how you go about reading this book. If you think that the first few chapters are not interesting to you and don't provide any value, feel free to skip them. You can also just read the whole book without ever writing a single line of code yourself. But I don't recommend that.

I would personally recommend you to read all the chapters in the right order because they built on top of each other. Of course, the code works without the theoretical understanding of the first chapter. But without it you will not be able to understand what you are doing and why it works or why it doesn't.

Also I highly recommend you to actively code along while reading this book. That's the only way you will understand the material. In the later chapters, there will be a lot of code. Read through it, understand it but also implement it yourself and play around with it. Experiment a little bit. What happens when you change some parameters? What happens when you add something? Try everything.

I think that's everything that needs to be said for now. I wish you a lot of success and fun while learning about neural networks in Python. I hope that this book will help you to progress in your career and life!

Just one little thing before we start. This book was written for you, so that you can get as much value as possible and learn to code effectively. If you find this book valuable or you think you have learned something new, please write a quick review on Amazon. It is completely free and takes about one minute. But it helps me produce more high quality books, which you can benefit from.

Thank you!

If you are interested in free educational content about programming and machine learning, check out: https://www.neuralnine.com/

1 – BASICS OF NEURAL NETWORKS

WHAT ARE NEURAL NETWORKS?

Before we start talking about how neural networks work, what types there are or how to work with them in Python, we should first clarify what neural networks actually are.

Artificial neural networks are mathematical structures that are inspired by the human brain. They consist of so-called *neurons*, which are interconnected with each other. The human brain consists of multiple billions of such neurons. Artificial neural networks use a similar principle.

INPUT   HIDDEN   OUTPUT

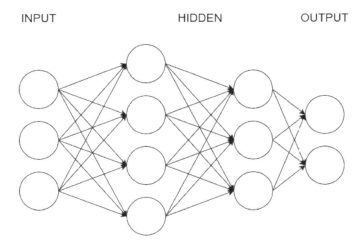

Fig. 1.1: Structure of an artificial neural network

The structure of a neural network is quite simple. In the figure above, we can see multiple layers. The first one is the *input layer* and the last one is the *output layer*. In between we have multiple so-called *hidden layers*.

The input layer is for the data that we want to feed into the neural network in order to get a result. Here we put all of the things that are "perceived" by or put into the neural network. For example, if we want to know if a picture shows a cat or a dog, we would put all the values of the individual pixels into the input layer. If we want to know if a person is overweight or not, we would enter parameters like height, weight etc.

The output layer then contains the results. There we can see the values generated by the neural network based on our inputs. For example the classification of an animal or a prediction value for something.

Everything in between are abstraction layers that we call hidden layers. These increase the complexity and the sophistication of the model and they expand the internal decision making. As a rule of thumb we could say that the more hidden layers and the more neurons we have, the more complex our model is.

STRUCTURE OF NEURONS

In order to understand how a neural network works, we need to understand how the individual neurons work.

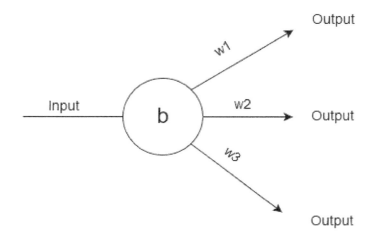

Fig. 1.2: Structure of an artificial neuron

As you can see every neuron gets a certain input, which is either the output of a previous neuron or the raw input of the input layer.

This input is a numerical value and it then gets multiplied by each individual *weight (w1, w2, w3...)*. At the end we then subtract the *bias (b)*. The result is the output of that particular connection. These outputs are that forwarded to the next layer of neurons.

What I just explained and what you can see at the figure above is an outdated version of a neuron, called the *perceptron*. Nowadays we are using much more complex neurons like the sigmoid neurons, which use mathematical functions to calculate the result for the output.

You can probably imagine how complex a system like this can get when all of the neurons are interconnected and influence each other. In between our input and output layer we oftentimes have numerous hidden layers with hundreds or thousands of neurons each. These abstraction layers then lead to a final result.

ACTIVATION FUNCTIONS

There are a lot of different so-called *activation functions* which make everything more complex. These functions determine the output of a neuron. Basically what we do is: We take the input of our neuron and feed the value into an activation function. This function then returns the output value. After that we still have our weights and biases.

SIGMOID ACTIVATION FUNCTION

A commonly used and popular activation function is the so-called *sigmoid activation function*. This function always returns a value between zero and one, no matter what the input is. The smaller the input, the closer the output will be to zero. The greater the input, the closer the output will be to one.

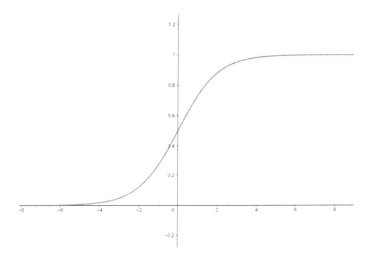

Fig 1.3: Sigmoid Activation Function

The mathematical formula looks like this:

$$f(x) = \frac{1}{1 + e^{-x}}$$

You don't have to understand this function 100% if you don't want to. But what you can easily see is that the one in the numerator indicates that the output will always lie in between zero and one, since the denominator is always positive. This function is much smoother than the basic perceptron.

RELU ACTIVATION FUNCTION

The probably most commonly used activation function is the so-called *ReLU function*. This stands for *rectified linear unit*. This function is very simple but also very useful. Whenever the input value is negative, it will return zero. Whenever it is positive, the output will just be the input.

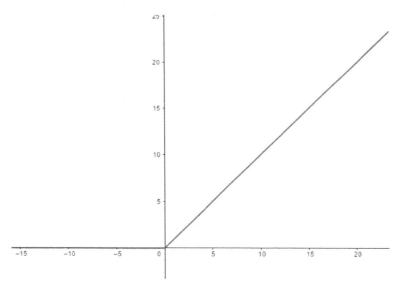

Fig 1.4: ReLU activation function

The mathematical formula looks like this:

$$f(x) = \max(0, x)$$

Even though that function is that simple, it oftentimes fulfils its purpose and it is commonly used as the go-to activation function for hidden layers.

Of course there are also a lot of other activation functions. But the purpose of this chapter is not to show you all of them but to give you a basic understanding of what activation functions are and how they work. We will talk about more activation functions in later chapters, when we are using them.

TYPES OF NEURAL NETWORKS

Neural networks are not only different because of the activation functions of their individual layers. There are also different types of layers and networks. In this book we are going to take a deeper look at these. For now, we will get a first overview of them in this chapter.

FEED FORWARD NEURAL NETWORKS

The so-called *feed forward neural networks* could be seen as the *classic* neural networks. Up until now we have primarily talked about these. In this type of network the information only flows into one direction – from the input layer to the output layer. There are no circles or cycles.

INPUT   HIDDEN   OUTPUT

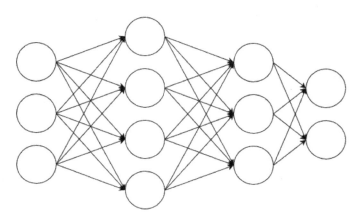

Fig 1.5: Feed Forward Neural Network

Above you can see the figure that we already talked about. If you look closer, you will see that the connections are pointed into one direction only. The information flows from left to right.

RECURRENT NEURAL NETWORKS

So-called *recurrent neural networks* on the other hand work differently. In these networks we have layers with neurons that not only connect to the neurons next layer but also to neurons of the previous or of their own layer. This can also be called *feedback*.

If we take the output of a neuron and use it as an input of the same neuron, we are talking about *direct feedback*. Connecting the output to neurons of the same layer is called *lateral feedback*. And if we take the output and feed it into neurons of the previous layer, we are talking about *indirect feedback*.

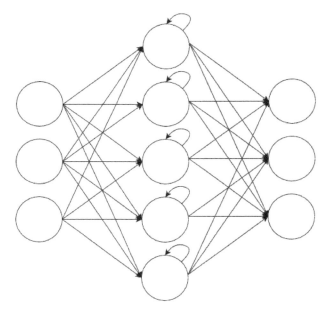

Fig. 1.6: Recurrent neural network (direct feedback)

The advantage of such a recurrent neural network is that it has a little memory and doesn't only take the immediate present data into account. We could say that it "looks back" a couple of iterations.

This kind of neural networks is oftentimes used when the tasks requires the processing of sequential data like text or speech. The feedback is very useful in this kind of tasks. However it is not very useful when dealing with image recognition or image processing.

CONVOLUTIONAL NEURAL NETWORKS

For this purpose we have the so-called *convolutional neural networks*. This type is primarily used for processing images and sound. It is especially useful when pattern recognition in noisy data is needed. This data may be image data, sound data or video data. It doesn't matter.

We are going to talk about how this type of neural network works in the respective chapter, but for now let us get a superficial quick overview.

Fig. 1.7: Xs and Os for classification

Let's look at a simple example. Here we have multiple Xs and Os as examples in a 16x16 pixels format. Each pixel is an input neuron and will be processed. At the end our neural network shall classify the image as either an X or an O.

Of course this example is trivial and could probably even be solved with a K-Nearest-Neighbors classification or a support vector machine. However, we are going to use it just to illustrate the principle.

For us humans it is very easy to differentiate between the two shapes. All of the Xs and all of the Os are quite similar. We easily spot the patterns. For a computer however, these images are totally different because the pixels do not match exactly. In this case, this is not a problem, but when we try to recognize cats and dogs, things get more complex.

What convolutional neural networks now do is: Instead of just looking at the individual pixels, they look for *patterns* or *features*.

Most of the Xs for example have a similar center with four pixels which splits up into four lines. Also they have long diagonal lines. Os on the other hand have an empty center and shorter lines. If we were classifying cats (in comparison with dogs) we could look for pointy ears or whiskers.

As I already said, this explanation is quite superficial and we are going to get into the details in the respective chapter. But what we basically do is just looking for the most important features and classifying the images based on these.

TRAINING AND TESTING

In order to make a neural network produce accurate results, we first need to train and test it. For this we use already classified data and split it up into training and testing data. Most of the time we will use 20% of the data for testing and 80% for training. The training data is the data that we use to optimize the performance. The testing data is data that the neural network has never seen before and we use it to verify that our model is accurate.

If we take the example of pictures of cats and dogs, we could take 8000 images that were classified by human experts and then show these to the neural network (we are going to talk about the technical details in a second). Then we could use 2000 images as testing data and compare the results of our neural network with the answers that we know to be true.

ERROR AND LOSS

When evaluating the accuracy or the performance of our model, we use two metrics – *error* and *loss*.

I am not going to get too deep and theoretical into the definition of these terms, since especially the concept of loss confuses a lot of people. Basically you could say that the error indicates how many of the examples were classified incorrectly. This is a relative value and it is expressed in percentages. An error of 0.21 for example would mean that 79% of the examples were classified correctly and 21% incorrectly. This metric is quite easy to understand for humans.

The loss on the other hand is a little bit more complex. Here we use a so-called *loss function* to determine the value. This value then indicates how bad our model is performing. Depending on the loss function, this value might look quite different. However, this is the value that we want to minimize in order to optimize our model.

GRADIENT DESCENT

The minimization of this value is done with the help of the so-called *gradient descent algorithm*. The mathematics behind this algorithm is quite confusing for a lot of people but I will do my best to explain it to you as simple as possible.

Imagine a loss function that looks like this (trivial example):

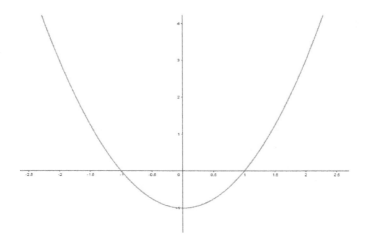

Fig 1.8: Trivial example for a loss function

Of course no loss function on earth would look like this because this doesn't make any sense at all. But we are going to use this function as an example to illustrate the concept of the gradient descent.

As I already said, our goal is to minimize the output of that function. This means that we are looking for the x-value which returns the lowest y-value. In this example, it is easy to see that this value is zero, which returns negative one. But how can our algorithm see this?

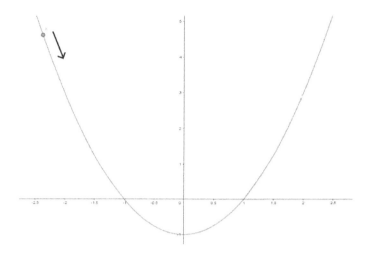

Fig. 1.9: Visualization of gradient descent

Since our computer doesn't see the graph like we do, it will just start with a random initial point A. We then calculate the gradient of the function in that particular point. This tells us in which direction we need to move in order to increase the output of the function the most. Since we want to minimize the output, we take a small step into the opposite direction. At the new point, in which we end up, we repeat this process. We continue to do this until we reach the valley where the gradient will be zero. This is the local minimum.

You can imagine it to be like a ball that rolls down the function's graph. It will inevitably roll into the local minimum. The emphasis is on *local*. Let's take a look at another function.

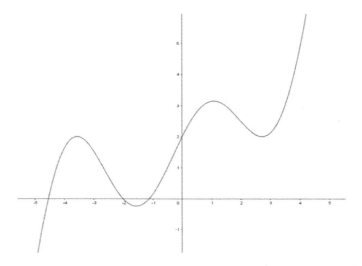

Fig. 1.10: Another trivial loss function example

The problem with this function is that it has multiple local minima. There is more than one valley. In which one we land depends on the initial starting point. In this case it might be easy to figure out which one is the best, but we will see in a second why this random approach doesn't work that easily.

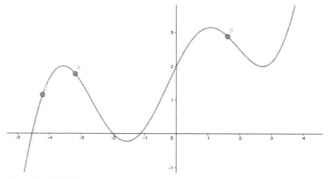

Fig. 1.11: Three different initial starting points

Here we can see three different starting points in the same function. When we start at point B, we will get into a local minimum but this local minimum is not even close to the minimum that we would get when starting at A. Also we have the starting point C, which might lead into an even lower minimum (if it leads into a minimum at all).

Multiple Features

Up until now the functions that we looked at, all had one input value and one output value. In a neural network however, we have thousands, if not more, weights, biases and other parameters, which we can tweak in order to change the outputs. The actual loss function gets the weights and biases as parameters and then returns the loss, based on the estimated and the actual results.

To get a better intuition about all of this, let us first take a look at a three-dimensional function.

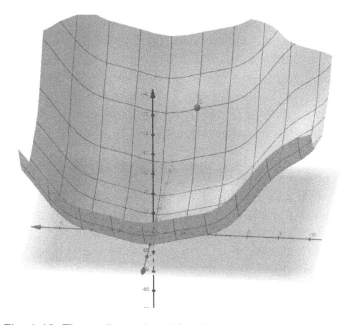

Fig. 1.12: Three-dimensional function

Here we apply the same principle. We have one point (this time in three dimensions) and this point shall roll down to the local minimum. The difference here is that we cannot only go left or right but into all directions of the plane. Therefore we need to determine the gradient for each axis. Mathematically speaking we need to work with partial derivatives.

First of all we look at the point and how the resulting value (vertical axis) changes, when we tweak the value of the first axis. Which direction is the one that causes the greatest increase of the output? We find this direction and then negate it, since we want to go the opposite way. We repeat the same process for the second input axis. At the end we take a tiny step into the resulting direction. This is the one with the steepest descent. Thus we inevitably roll into the local minimum.

Now try to imagine that process in multiple thousands of dimensions. Each weight and each bias would be one axis and therefore one additional dimension. Our algorithm needs to tweak all of these parameters in order to produce the best possible output. Of course as humans we can't imagine anything that is higher than three or four dimensions, let alone visualize it.

The Mathematics

We are not going to get too deep into the mathematics here but it might be quite beneficial for you to get a little bit more familiar with the mathematical notations.

Let's imagine our loss function to be the following one:

$$C(w, b) = \frac{1}{2n} * \sum_{x} ||f(x) - y||^2$$

What this function basically does is the following: We pass the weights and biases as parameters. Then we calculate all the differences between the predictions of the models and the actually desired results. In this case $f(x)$ is the prediction of the network and y is the actual result. We calculate the absolute value of the difference so that we are dealing with a positive value. Then we square that difference. We do this for every single example and we add all the differences up so that we get the sum. At the end we then divide it by twice the amount of examples.

Let me explain it again a little bit simpler. We take all the differences, square them, sum them up and divide it by twice the amount of examples in order to get the *mean squared error*. This is also the name of this loss function.

Now we want to minimize the output of this function, by tweaking the parameters with the gradient descent.

$$\nabla C = \left(\frac{\partial C}{\partial v_1}, \frac{\partial C}{\partial v_2}, \dots, \frac{\partial C}{\partial v_n}\right)$$

We want to calculate the gradient of this function. This gradient is composed of all the partial derivatives of the loss function C (stands for the alternative name of *cost function*). The vectors v1, v2 etc. are the vectors of the individual weights and biases.

The only thing that we need to do now is to make a tiny step into the opposite direction of that gradient.

$$-\nabla C * \varepsilon$$

We take the negative gradient and multiply it with a minimal value.

Don't panic if you don't understand everything about the mathematics. The focus of this book is the application of these principles. Therefore you can continue reading even if you don't understand the mathematics at all.

BACKPROPAGATION

We now understand what is needed to optimize our neural network. The question remains though, how we are going to implement all of that. How are we going to calculate the gradient? How are we going to tweak the parameters? For this we are going to use the *backpropagation algorithm*. Here I will also try to explain everything as simple as possible.

Basically backpropagation is just the algorithm that calculates the gradient for the gradient descent algorithm. It determines how and how much we need to change which parameters in order to get a better result.

First of all we take the prediction of the model and compare it to the actually desired result.

Prediction   Desired Result

Fig. 1.13: Comparing the outputs

What we see in the figure above is the comparison of the output layer (consisting of two neurons) and the desired results. Let's say the first neuron is the one that indicates that the picture is a cat. In this case the prediction would say that the picture is a dog (since the second neuron has a higher activation) but the picture is actually one of a cat.

So we look at how the results need to be changed in order to fit the actual data. Notice however that we don't have any direct influence on the output of the neurons. We can only control the weights and the biases.

We now know that we want to increase the value of the first neuron and decrease the value of the second neuron. For this we will need to look back one layer.

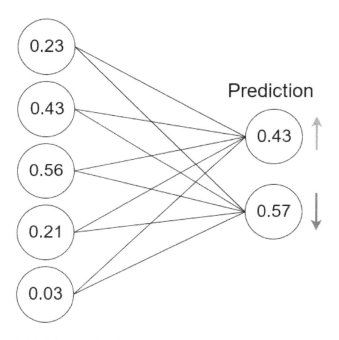

Fig. 1.14: Looking back one layer

In order to change the value of neurons we can either tweak the weights and biases or we can try to change the inputs.

Let's take a look at how the value of the final output neurons gets calculated. We will notice that some connections increase this value, whereas some connections decrease it. Put differently: There are some neurons in the previous layer that will, when tweaked into a certain direction, change the value of the output neurons towards the desired results.

So we now again think, how the value of each neuron should be changed in order to move towards the desired result. Keep in mind that we still cannot directly influence these values. We can only control the weights and biases but it still makes sense to think about the ideal changes that we would like to make.

Also keep in mind that up until now everything we are doing is just for a single training example. We will have to look at every single training example and how this example will want to change all these values. This has to be done for multiple thousands of examples. What we are actually doing is therefore determining the change that is the best for all the training examples at once. Basically the mean or average.

For example if 7000 examples want a certain neuron to have a higher value and 3000 examples want it to have a lower value, we will increase it but not as much as we would increase it if 10,000 examples demanded it.

When we do this for every single neuron of that layer, we know how we need to change each of those. Now we need to go back one more layer and repeat the same process. We do this until we get to the input layer.

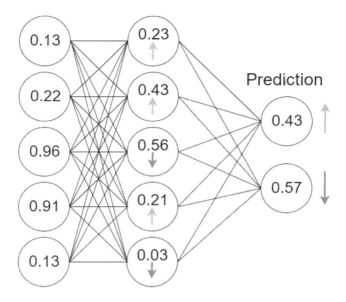

Fig. 1.15: One more layer back

When we continue to do this process until we reach the input layer, we will get the on average demanded changes for all weights and biases. This is the exact same thing as the negative gradient of the gradient descent algorithm. We then take a tiny step and repeat the whole process. Depending on the machine we are working on and some other parameters this might take a while. We do this over and over again until we are satisfied with the results.

SUMMARY

Since we covered a lot of different theoretical topics in this chapter, let us summarize the essential things:

- Activation functions determine the activation of a neuron which then influences the outputs.
- The classic neural networks are feed forward neural networks. The information only flows into one direction.
- In recurrent neural networks we work with feedback and it is possible to take the output of future layers as the input of neurons. This creates something like a memory.
- Convolutional neural networks are primarily used for images, audio data and other data which requires pattern recognition. They split the data into features.
- Usually we use 80% of the data we have as training data and 20% as testing data.
- The error indicates how much percent of the data was classified incorrectly.
- The loss is a numerical value which is calculated with a loss function. This is the value that we want to minimize in order to optimize our model.
- For the minimization of the output we use the gradient descent algorithm. It finds the local minimum of a function.
- Backpropagation is the algorithm which calculates the gradient for the gradient descent algorithm. This is done by starting from the output layer and reverse engineering the desired changes.

2 – Installing Libraries

Development Environment

Now after all that theory, let us get into the implementation. First of all, we are going to set up our development environment. Actually it is your choice which IDE you are going to use. However I highly recommend using a professional environment like PyCharm or Jupyter Notebook.

PyCharm:
https://www.jetbrains.com/pycharm/download/

Anaconda: https://www.anaconda.com/distribution/

Libraries

Also, we are going to need some external libraries for our projects. It is important that we understand all the theory behind neural networks but it is a waste of time to reinvent the wheel and code everything from scratch. Therefore we will use professional libraries that do most of the work for us.

For this book we will need Tensorflow, which is the most popular library for working with neural networks. We will use *pip* for the installation:

```
pip install tensorflow
```

In the course of this book we will also oftentimes use some of the external libraries that we have already used in the previous volumes. If we use additional libraries, we are going to mention that an installation is needed in the respective chapter. The following libraries are yet pretty important and should be part of the stack of every Python programmer.

```
pip install numpy
```

```
pip install matplotlib
```

```
pip install pandas
```

All these libraries will do a lot of the work for us. We almost don't have to deal with any mathematics or theory at all. With these libraries we are operating at the use-case level.

3 – Handwritten Digit Recognition

Let us now finally get into some real programming. In this chapter our goal is to build and train a neural network, which recognizes handwritten digits with a mind-blowing accuracy. It will be able to recognize the digits from 0 to 9.

Required Libraries

For this chapter we will need the following imports:

```
import cv2
import numpy as np
import tensorflow as tf
import matplotlib.pyplot as plt
```

Tensorflow is the main library here. We will use it to load data sets, build neural networks, train them etc. The other three libraries are not necessary for the functionality of the neural network. We are only using them in order to load our own images of digits at the end.

Numpy will be used for reformatting our own images and *Matplotlib* will be used for their visualization.

CV2 is the *OpenCV* library and it will allow us to load our images into the script. You will need to install this module separately:

```
pip install opencv-python
```

LOADING AND PREPARING DATA

Before we start building and using our neural network, we need to first get some training data and prepare it.

For this chapter we are going to use the *MNIST dataset* which contains 60,000 training examples and 10,000 testing examples of handwritten digits that are already classified correctly. These images have a resolution of 28x28 pixels. We will use the *keras* module, in order to load the dataset.

```
mnist = tf.keras.datasets.mnist
(X_train, y_train), (X_test, y_test) =
mnist.load_data()
```

In order to get the dataset, we access the *mnist* object from the *keras.datasets*. Then we call the *load_data* function. This function automatically splits the data appropriately and returns a tuple with the training data and a tuple with the testing data.

In order to make the whole data easier to process, we are going to *normalize* it. This means that we scale down all the values so that they end up between 0 and 1.

```
X_train = tf.keras.utils.normalize(X_train,
axis=1)
X_test = tf.keras.utils.normalize(X_test,
axis=1)
```

For this we use the *normalize* function of *keras.utils*. We have now structured and normalized our data so that we can start building our neural network.

BUILDING THE NEURAL NETWORK

Let's think about what kind of structure would make sense for our task. Since we are dealing with images, it would be reasonable to build a convolutional neural network. When we take a look at the official website of the MNIST dataset we will find a table of the various different types and structures of neural networks and how well they perform at this task.

MNIST Website: http://yann.lecun.com/exdb/mnist/

There we can see that in fact convolutional neural networks are one of the best ways to do this. However we are going to use an ordinary feed forward neural network for this task. First of all, because it is certainly enough and second of all, because we will come back to convolutional neural networks in a later chapter. It makes sense to start with the fundamental structures first.

```
model = tf.keras.models.Sequential()
```

We use the *models* module from *keras* to create a new neural network. The *Sequential* constructor does this for us. Now we have a model, which doesn't have any layers in it. Those have to be added manually.

```
model.add(tf.keras.layers.Flatten(input_shape=(28
,28)))
```

We start out by adding a so-called *Flatten* layer as
our first layer. In order to add a layer to our model,
we use the *add* function. Then we can choose the
kind of layer that we want from the *layers* module. As
you can see, we specified an input shape of 28x28
which represents the resolution of the images. What
a flattened layer basically does is it flattens the input
and makes it one dimensional. So instead of a 28x28
grid, we end up with 784 neurons lined up. Our goal
is now to get to the right result based on these pixels.

```
model.add(tf.keras.layers.Dense(units=128,
activation=tf.nn.relu))
model.add(tf.keras.layers.Dense(units=128,
activation=tf.nn.relu))
```

In the next step we now add two *Dense* layers.
These are our hidden layers and increase the
complexity of our model. Both layers have 128
neurons each. The activation function is the *ReLU*
function (see chapter 1). Dense layers connect every
neuron of this layer with all the neurons of the next
and previous layer. It is basically just a default layer.

```
model.add(tf.keras.layers.Dense(units=10,
activation=tf.nn.softmax))
```

Last but not least we add an output layer. This one is
also a dense layer but it only has ten neurons and a
different activation function. The values of the ten
neurons indicate how much our model believes that
the respective number is the right classification. The

first neuron is for the zero, the second for the one and so on.

The activation function that we use here is the *softmax* function. This function scales the output values so that they all add up to one. Thus it transforms the absolute values into relative values. Every neuron then indicates how likely it is that this respective number is the result. We are dealing with percentages.

```
model = tf.keras.models.Sequential()
model.add(tf.keras.layers.Flatten(input_shape=(28,28
)))
model.add(tf.keras.layers.Dense(units=128,
activation=tf.nn.relu))
model.add(tf.keras.layers.Dense(units=128,
activation=tf.nn.relu))
model.add(tf.keras.layers.Dense(units=10,
activation=tf.nn.softmax))
```

In a nutshell, we have a flattened input layer with 784 neurons for the input pixels, followed by two hidden layers and one output layer with the probabilities for each digit.

COMPILING THE MODEL

Before we start training and testing our model, we need to compile it first. This optimizes it and we can also choose a loss function.

```
model.compile(optimizer='adam',
loss='sparse_categorical_crossentropy',
metrics=['accuracy'])
```

We are not going to get too deep into the optimizers and the loss functions here. The parameters that we chose here are pretty good for our task. Also, we define the metrics that we are interested in. In this case, we only care about the accuracy of our model.

TRAINING AND TESTING

Now we get to the essential part of the whole project – the training and testing. For this, we just have to use the *fit* function of our model.

```
model.fit(X_train, y_train, epochs=3)
```

Here we pass our x- and y-values as the training data. Then we also define the number of epochs that we want to go through. This number defines how many times our model is going to see the same data over and over again.

```
loss, accuracy = model.evaluate(X_test, y_test)
print(loss)
print(accuracy)
```

After that we use the *evaluate* method and pass our testing data, to determine the accuracy and the loss. Most of the time we get an accuracy of around 95% (try it yourself). This is pretty good if you take into account that mere guessing would give us a 10% chance of being right. Our model performs quite well.

```
model.save('digits.model')
```

Instead of training the model over and over again every single time we run the script, we can save it and load it later on. We do this by using the *save* method and specifying a name.

```
model =
tf.keras.models.load_model('digits.model')
```

If we now want to load the model, we can just use the *load_model* function of *keras.models* and refer to the same name.

CLASSIFYING YOUR OWN DIGITS

Now that we know that our model works and performs quite well, let us try to predict our own handwritten digits. For this you can either use a program like Paint, and set the resolution to 28x28 pixels, or you can actually use a scanner, scan a real digit and scale the picture down to that format.

```
img = cv2.imread('digit.png')[:,:,0]
img = np.invert(np.array([img]))
```

In order to load our image into the script, we use the *imread* function of OpenCV. We specify the file name and use the index slicing at the end in order to choose just one dimension, in order to fit the format. Also we need to invert the image and convert it into a NumPy array. This is necessary because otherwise it will see the image as white on black rather than black on white. That would confuse our model.

```
prediction = model.predict(img)
print("Prediction:
{}".format(np.argmax(prediction)))
plt.imshow(img[0])
plt.show()
```

Now we use the *predict* method to make a prediction for our image. This prediction consists of the ten activations from the output neurons. Since we need to generate a result out of that, we are going to use the *argmax* function. This function returns the index of the highest value. In this case this is equivalent to the digit with the highest probability or activation. We can then visualize that image with the *imshow* method of Matplotlib and print the prediction.

Prediction: 7

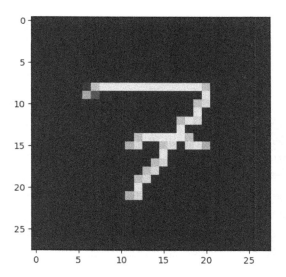

Fig. 2.1: Classified Digit 7

Even though our model is pretty accurate it might still make some mistakes, especially if you tend to write digits in a very unusual way. However this example should have helped you to better understand neural networks and also to get a feeling of how to work with them in Python.

4 – GENERATING TEXTS

In machine learning we are oftentimes dealing with sequential data. Not every input is looked at separately but in context of the previous data.

RECURRENT NEURAL NETWORKS

We already mentioned that for these kinds of tasks, recurrent neural networks are the best choice. Remember: Recurrent layers not only forward their output to the next layer but can also send it to their own or to the previous layer.

This type of network is therefore especially effective when we are dealing with time-dependent data. Examples for this are weather data, stock prices and other values that change sequentially.

In this chapter however we are going to focus on the generation of texts. Texts can also be seen as sequential data, since after every combination of letters a certain "next letter" follows. So here we are not just looking at the last one letter but at the last 20 or 30 letters.

What we want to do here is to get our neural network to generate texts similar to those of the famous poet Shakespeare. For this we are just going to show our model original texts and then train it to generate similar texts itself.

LONG-SHORT-TERM MEMORY (LSTM)

When we talked about recurrent neural networks in the first chapter, we looked at the most basic version of recurrent neurons. These were ordinary neurons that were just connected to themselves or to neurons of the previous layer.

These are definitely useful but for our purposes another type is better suited. For this task we are going to use so-called *LSTM neurons*. This stands for *Long-Short-Term Memory* and indicates that these neurons have some sort of retention.

The problem with ordinary recurrent neurons is that they might forget important information because they don't have any reliable mechanisms that prioritize information based on relevance. Let's look at a quick example. Read the following review of a product:

Awesome! This drink tastes wonderful and reminds me of a mixture of kiwis and strawberries. I only drank half of it but I will definitely buy it again!

When you read this review and you want to tell a friend about it in a couple of days, you will definitely not remember every single word of it. You will forget a lot of words like "I", "will" or "this" and their position, unless you read the text multiple times and try to memorize it.

Primarily you will remember the terms like "awesome", "wonderful", "mixture of kiwis and strawberries" and "definitely buy it again". This is because these are the essential words. And an LSTM network does the same thing. It filters out the unimportant information and only remembers the essential content. These words and phrases are the most important things to look at, in order to determine if this review is positive or negative. Words like "I", "will" or "this" may also appear in a negative review.

We are not going to talk too much about the detailed workings of LSTMs. This would be too much for this chapter and this book. For our purposes it is important to understand that LSTMs have mechanisms that focus on the retention of the essential data. Therefore we use these neurons instead of the default recurrent neurons.

LOADING SHAKESPEARE'S TEXTS

As I already mentioned, we are going to need a decent amount of Shakespeare's texts, in order to train our model. Thus we will now start to load this data into the script. We are going to use the file that is also used by the official Tensorflow Keras tutorials.

Link: https://bit.ly/37IjtMs

This is a shortened link to the file. However, don't bother downloading it manually, since we are going to load it directly into the script, using the full link.

Of course, you can also use all kinds of different text files here. You can export WhatsApp chats and use them as training data, you can download speeches of Donald Trump and use these. Feel free to use whatever you like. The output will then be similar to the training data.

For this chapter we will need the following imports:

```
import random
import numpy as np
import tensorflow as tf
from tensorflow.keras.models import Sequential
from tensorflow.keras.optimizers import RMSprop
from tensorflow.keras.layers import Activation, Dense,
LSTM
```

We are going to talk about the individual classes and modules, when we use them. The first step is to now download the file.

```
filepath =
tf.keras.utils.get_file('shakespeare.txt',
'https://storage.googleapis.com/download.tensorflow.
org/data/shakespeare.txt')

text = open(filepath, 'rb')\
    .read().decode(encoding='utf-8').lower()
```

We use the *get_file* method of *keras.utils* in order to download the file. The first parameter is the filename that we choose and the second one is the link. After that we open the file, decode it and save it into a variable. Notice that we are using the *lower* function at the end. We do this because it drastically increases the performance, since we have much less possible characters to choose from. And for the semantics of the text the case is irrelevant.

PREPARING DATA´

The problem that we have right now with our data is that we are dealing with text. We cannot just train a neural network on letters or sentences. We need to convert all of these values into numerical data. So we have to come up with a system that allows us to convert the text into numbers, to then predict specific numbers based on that data and then again convert the resulting numbers back into text.

Also I am not going to use the whole text file as training data. If you have the capacities or the time to train your model on the whole data, do it! It will produce much better results. But if your machine is slow or you have limited time, you might consider just using a part of the text.

```
text = text[300000:800000]
```

Here we select all the characters from character number 300,000 up until 800,000. So we are processing a total of 500,000 characters, which should be enough for pretty decent results.

CONVERTING TEXT

Now we need to start building a system, which allows us to convert characters into numbers and numbers into characters. We are not going to use the ASCII codes but our own indices.

```
characters = sorted(set(text))
```

```
char_to_index = dict((c, i) for i, c in
enumerate(characters))
index_to_char = dict((i, c) for i, c in
enumerate(characters))
```

We create a sorted set of all the unique characters that occur in the text. In a set no value appears more than once, so this is a good way to filter out the characters. After that we define two structures for converting the values. Both are dictionaries that enumerate the characters. In the first one, the characters are the keys and the indices are the values. In the second one it is the other way around. Now we can easily convert a character into a unique numerical representation and vice versa. Notice that the *enumerate* function doesn't use the ASCII values but just indexes every single character.

SPLITTING TEXT

In this next step, we will need to split our text into sequences, which we can use for training. For this, we will define a sequence length and a step size.

```
SEQ_LENGTH = 40
STEP_SIZE = 3

sentences = []
next_char = []
```

Our goal is to create a list of multiple sequences and another list of all the "next characters" that follow these sequences. In this case, we chose a sequence length of 40 and a step size of three. This means that our base sentences will be 40 characters long and that we will jump three characters from the start of one sentence in order to get to the start of the next sentence. A step size that is too small might result in too many similar examples where as a step size that is too large might cause bad performance. When choosing the sequence length we must also try to find a number that produces sentences that are long enough but also not too long so that our model doesn't rely on too much previous data.

Now we are going to fill up the two empty lists that we just created. These will be the features and the targets of our training data. The text sequences will be the input or the features and the next characters will be the results or the targets.

```
for i in range(0, len(text) - SEQ_LENGTH,
STEP_SIZE):
    sentences.append(text[i: i + SEQ_LENGTH])
    next_char.append(text[i + SEQ_LENGTH])
```

Here we run a for loop and iterate over our text with the given sequence length and step size. The control variable *i* gets increased by *STEP_SIZE* with each iteration.

Additionally, in every iteration, we add the sequence from *i* up to *i* plus the sequence length, to our list. In our case we start with the first 40 characters, save them, then shift the start by three characters, save the next 40 characters and so on. Also we save every "next character" into our second list.

CONVERT TO NUMPY FORMAT

This training data now needs to be converted into numerical values and then into NumPy arrays.

```
x = np.zeros((len(sentences), SEQ_LENGTH,
              len(characters)), dtype=np.bool)
y = np.zeros((len(sentences),
              len(characters)), dtype=np.bool)
```

For this we first create two NumPy arrays full of zeroes. These zeroes however are actually *False* values, because our data type is *bool* which stands for *Boolean*. The *x* array is three-dimensional and it shapes is based on the amount of sentences, the length of those and the amount of possible characters. In this array we store the information about which character appears at which position in which sentence. Wherever a character occurs, we will set the respective value to one or *True*.

The *y* array for the targets is two-dimensional and its shape is based on the amount of sentences and the amount of possible characters. Here we also work with bools. When a character is the next character for a given sentence, we set the position to one or *True*. Now we need to fill up these two arrays with the proper values.

```
for i, satz in enumerate(sentences):
    for t, char in enumerate(satz):
        x[i, t, char_to_index[char]] = 1
    y[i, char_to_index[next_char[i]]] = 1
```

This code does exactly what I just described above. We use the enumerate function two times so that we know which indices we need to mark with a one. Here we use our *char_to_index* dictionary, in order to get the right index for each character.

To make all of that a little bit more clear, let us look at an example. Let's say the character 'g' has gotten the index 17. If this character now occurs in the third sentence (which means index two), at the fourth positon (which means index three), we would set *x[2,3,17]* to one.

BUILD RECURRENT NEURAL NETWORK

Now our training data is perfectly prepared and has the right format that our neural network can work with. But this network has to be built yet. Let's look at the needed imports again and talk a little bit about their role:

```
import random
import numpy as np
import tensorflow as tf
from tensorflow.keras.models import Sequential
from tensorflow.keras.optimizers import RMSprop
from tensorflow.keras.layers import Activation, Dense,
LSTM
```

The library *random* will be used later on in a helper function. We have already used *numpy*. We used the basic *tensorflow* library was used to load the data from the internet.

For building our neural network, we will once again need the *Sequential* model from Keras. This time however, we will use a different optimizer, namely the *RMSprop*. And of course we also import the layer types, which we are going to use.

```
model = Sequential()
model.add(LSTM(128,
               input_shape=(SEQ_LENGTH,
                             len(characters))))
model.add(Dense(len(characters)))
model.add(Activation('softmax'))
```

Our model is actually quite simple. The inputs go directly into an *LSTM* layer with 128 neurons. We define the input shape to be the sequence length times the amount of possible characters. We already talked about how this layer works. This layer is the memory of our model. It is then followed by a *Dense* layer with as many neurons as we have possible characters. This is our hidden layer. That adds complexity and abstraction to our network. And then last but not least we have the output layer, which is an *Activation* layer. In this case it once again uses the *softmax* function that we know from the last chapter.

```
model.compile(loss='categorical_crossentropy',
              optimizer=RMSprop(lr=0.01))

model.fit(x, y, batch_size=256, epochs=4)
```

Now we compile our model and optimize it. We choose a learning rate of 0.01. After that we *fit* our model on the training data that we prepared. Here we choose a *batch_size* of 256 and four *epochs*. The batch size indicates how many sentences we are going to show the model at once.

HELPER FUNCTION

The model is now trained and ready to generate some predictions. However, the output that we get is not really satisfying. What our network gives us as a result is actually just the next character in the numerical format.

```python
def sample(preds, temperature=1.0):
    preds = np.asarray(preds).astype('float64')
    preds = np.log(preds) / temperature
    exp_preds = np.exp(preds)
    preds = exp_preds / np.sum(exp_preds)
    probas = np.random.multinomial(1, preds, 1)
    return np.argmax(probas)
```

I copied this function from the official Keras tutorial.

Link: https://keras.io/examples/lstm_text_generation/

This function will later on take the predictions of our model as a parameter and then choose a "next character". The second parameter *temperature* indicates how risky or how unusual the pick shall be. A low value will cause a conservative pick, whereas a high value will cause a more experimental pick. We will use this helper function in our final function.

GENERATING TEXTS

The neural network that we have returns as a result an array with bool values. From those we need to extract the choice using our helper function. But then we still end up with a numerical value which represents just one character. So we need to convert this number into a readable representation and we also need to produce not just one "next character" but multiple.

```python
def generate_text(length, temperature):
    start_index = random.randint(0, len(text) - SEQ_LENGTH - 1)
    generated = ''
    sentence = text[start_index: start_index + SEQ_LENGTH]
    generated += sentence
    for i in range(length):
        x_predictions = np.zeros((1, SEQ_LENGTH, len(characters)))
        for t, char in enumerate(sentence):
            x_predictions[0, t, char_to_index[char]] = 1

        predictions = model.predict(x_predictions, verbose=0)[0]
        next_index = sample(predictions,
                            temperature)
        next_character = index_to_char[next_index]

        generated += next_character
        sentence = sentence[1:] + next_character
    return generated
```

This is the function that we are going to use for that. It looks more complicated than it actually is. So don't panic. We will analyze it step-by-step. First we generate a random entry point into our text. This is important because our network needs some starting sequence in order to generate characters. So the first part will be copied from the original text. If you want to have text that is completely generated, you can cut the first characters out of the string afterwards.

We then convert this initial text again into a NumPy array. After that we feed these x-values into our neural network and predict the output. For this we use the *predict* method. This will output the probabilities for the next characters. We then take these predictions and pass them to our helper function. You have probably noticed that we also have a *temperature* parameter in this function. We directly pass that to the helper function.

In the end we receive a choice from the *sample* function in numerical format. This choice needs to be converted into a readable character, using our second dictionary. Then we add this character to our generated text and repeat this process until we reach the desired length.

RESULTS

Let's take a look at some samples. I played around with the parameters, in order to diversify the results. I am not going to show you all of the results, but just some snippets that I found interesting.

```
print(generate_text(300, 0.2))
print(generate_text(300, 0.4))
print(generate_text(300, 0.5))
print(generate_text(300, 0.6))
```

```
print(generate_text(300, 0.7))
print(generate_text(300, 0.8))
```

Settings: *Length: 300, Temperature: 0.4 (Conservative)*

ay, marry, thou dost the more thou dost the mornish,
and if the heart of she gentleman, or will,
the heart with the serving a to stay thee,
i will be my seek of the sould stay stay
the fair thou meanter of the crown of manguar;
the send their souls to the will to the breath:
the wry the sencing with the sen

Settings: *Length: 300, Temperature: 0.6 (Medium)*

warwick:
and, thou nast the hearth by the createred
to the daughter, that he word the great enrome;
that what then; if thou discheak, sir.

clown:
sir i have hath prance it beheart like!

Settings: *Length: 300, Temperature: 0.8 (Experimental)*

i hear him speak.
what! can so young a thordo, word appeal thee,
but they go prife with recones, i thou dischidward!

---

has thy noman, lookly comparmal to had
ester,
and, my seatiby bedath, romeo, thou lauke
be;
how will i have so the gioly beget discal
bone.

clown:
i have seemitious in the step--by this low,

As you can see, the results are far away from perfection. But considering the fact that our computer doesn't even understand what words or sentences are, this is quite impressive nevertheless. Most sentences don't make a lot of sense and you can find some made up words but the texts are unique and it learned to generate those just by reading some Shakespeare literature.

Now it is your turn! Experiment around with that code. Tweak the parameters. Use different training texts. Maybe you want to export your WhatsApp chats and train the model on those. The text you use for training drastically influences the final generated texts.

5 – IMAGE AND OBJECT RECOGNITION

In the first chapter we talked about convolutional neural networks and the fact that this type of neural network is especially effective when processing image and sound data. They excel at recognizing patterns and segmenting the data into so-called *features*. Thus they perform much better than ordinary feed forward neural networks.

WORKINGS OF CNNS

Convolutional neural networks derive their name from the fact that they consist of *convolutional layers*. These oftentimes followed by *pooling layers*, which filter the resulting information and simplify it. A convolutional neural network may consist of multiple such combinations. For example, we could have an input layer, followed by a convolutional layer, followed by a pooling layer and this combination repeats three times. After that we add a couple of dense layers at the end and a final output layer.

CONVOLUTIONAL LAYER

Similar to an ordinary layer, convolutional layers also get their input from previous neurons, process it and send the result to the next layer. The processing of convolutional layers is called *convolution*. We are going to talk about this in a second.

Most of the time convolutional layers are two- or three-dimensional. When we load black-and-white images and classify those, we are dealing with two dimensions. Working with colored images happens in three dimensions. The individual values represent the pixels.

Let's take a superficial look at how such a processing could look like.

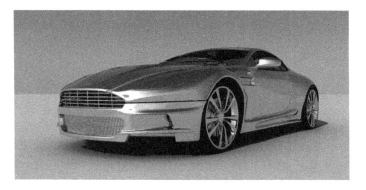

Fig. 5.1: Image of a car

When you look at this picture, you immediately recognize that it shows a car. This is because you have already seen numerous cars throughout your whole life and you now the label "car". For a computer that isn't so obvious. If we have ten possible objects for classification (car, plane, cat, dog, table etc.), it will be impossible for it, to classify these objects by nature.

With ordinary feed forward neural networks it would just look at all the pixels, try to make some connections and then make a prediction, which will probably be inaccurate. What works when it comes to handwritten digits doesn't work as easily in more complicated examples. Handwritten digits are just clear shapes, black on white. Images of a car or a dog can be shot from different perspectives on different backgrounds with different colors. Sometimes the pictures will be brighter and sometimes darker. This will inevitably confuse an ordinary neural network.

What stays the same though, are all the features, attributes and patterns of those objects. A car has tires, wheels, side mirrors, a windshield etc. The perspective might always be different but most of the features can always be found. And this is exactly what convolutional neural networks do. They extract the relevant features from the images.

Fig. 5.2: Example of feature extraction

When you think about it, this is the exact same process that we humans do. We don't look at every single "pixel" of our field of view. Instead we look at the big picture and recognize the features of a car. We see wheels, a license plate, the shape and before we even have time to think about it, we know that what we see is a car.

Let's get a little bit deeper into the technical details of convolutional layers. Fundamentally a convolutional layer is just a matrix that we apply onto our data.

0.762	0.561	0.022
0.675	0.132	0.982
0.111	0.671	0.231

We will take this 3x3 Matrix as an example. This matrix is now our filter or our convolutional layer. Additionally we can also imagine a picture which is encoded in the same way. Each pixel would have a value in between 0 and 1. The higher the value, the brighter the pixel and the lower the value, the darker the pixel would be. Zero would then equal black and one would equal white.

What we now do is we apply our matrix onto each 3x3 field of our image. Applying it means calculating the scalar product of both matrices. We take the first 3x3 pixels of our image and calculate the scalar product with our filter. Then we shift our selection by one column and apply the same operation to the next 3x3 pixels. The scalar product is then the new resulting pixel.

Now you are probably asking yourself two questions. First of all: Why are we doing all of that? And second of all: Where do we get the values for our filter from? The answer to both of this question is kind of the same.

Initially we use random and irrelevant values. Therefore the filtering has no real effect in the beginning. But we are operating in the world of machine learning. So we start filtering our images with random values. Then we look at the results and evaluate the accuracy of our model. Of course it is going to be quite low. Thus we tweak the parameters using backpropagation over and over again, so that our results approve. This works because our filters become pattern detectors over time because of all this training. When certain patterns occur over and over again in different pictures, the respective values in our filters and channels will be accordingly high.

Most of the time these filters are not 3x3 matrices but 64x64 matrices or even bigger ones. And a convolutional layer consists of multiple such filters. Also, we oftentimes line up many convolutional layers in a row. Thus, everything gets kind of complex and sophisticated and very effective.

POOLING LAYER

Pooling layers are the layers that usually follow convolutional layers. Their primary role is to simplify the output of those. Roughly speaking we could say that these layers make sure that our model is focusing on the essential parts before we forward our data even further.

The most popular type of pooling is the so-called *max-pooling*. Here we take 2x2 matrices of our images and only take on the one highest value for further processing.

Pooling reduces the required space, increases the computational speed and counteracts overfitting. In general it saves resources without causing worse performance.

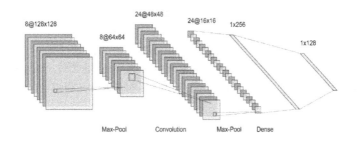

Fig. 5.3: Structure of a convolutional neural network

Here we see what a convolutional neural network could look like. Initially the inputs flow into a convolutional layer which uses eight 128x128 filters. The result is then forwarded into a max-pooling layer which reduces it to its essential parts. After that we repeat the process with two more layers in a smaller resolution. Then we feed the information into two dense layers and end up with a final classification.

LOAD AND PREPARE IMAGE DATA

Let us now get to the implementation part of the chapter. In this chapter we are going to use another Keras dataset, which contains numerous images of ten different categories. These are the following:

```
['Plane', 'Car', 'Bird', 'Cat', 'Deer',
'Dog', 'Frog', 'Horse', 'Ship', 'Truck']
```

This dataset contains tens of thousands of images of different objects with their respective class. Our goal here is to train a convolutional neural network on that data, in order to then classify other images that the model has never seen before.

For this we will need the following libraries:

```
import cv2 as cv
import numpy as np
import matplotlib.pyplot as plt
from tensorflow.keras import datasets, layers,
models
```

If haven't installed OpenCV yet, you need to do this. For this just open your command line and enter:


```
pip install opencv-python
```

We again receive the data already split up into two tuples, when we load it from Keras.

```
(train_images, train_labels), (test_images,
test_labels) = datasets.cifar10.load_data()
train_images, test_images =
train_images / 255.0, test_images / 255.0
```

This time we load the *cifat10* dataset with the *load_data* method. We also normalize this data immediately after that, by dividing all values by 255. Since we are dealing with RGB values, and all values lie in between 0 and 255, we end up with values in between 0 and 1.

Next, we define the possible class names in a list, so that we can label the final numerical results later on. The neural network will again produce a softmax result, which means that we will use the *argmax* function, to figure out the class name.

```
class_names = ['Plane', 'Car', 'Bird', 'Cat',
'Deer',
               'Dog', 'Frog', 'Horse', 'Ship',
'Truck']
```

Now we can visualize a section of the data, to see what this dataset looks like.

```
for i in range(16):
    plt.subplot(4,4,i+1)
    plt.xticks([])
    plt.yticks([])
    plt.imshow(train_images[i],
cmap=plt.cm.binary)
    plt.xlabel(class_names[train_labels[i][0]])

plt.show()
```

For this we run a for loop with 16 iterations and create a 4x4 grid of subplots. The x-ticks and the y-ticks will be set to empty lists, so that we don't have annoying coordinates. After that, we use the *imshow* method, to visualize the individual images. The label of the image will then be the respective class name.

Fig. 5.4: Images of the Cifar10 dataset with labels

This dataset contains a lot of images. If your computer is not high-end or you don't want to spend too much time on training the model, I suggest you only use a part of the data for training.

```
train_images = train_images[:20000]
train_labels = train_labels[:20000]
test_images = test_images[:4000]
test_labels = test_labels[:4000]
```

Here for example we only use the first 20,000 of the training images and the first 4,000 of the test images. Of course your model will be way more accurate if you use all the images. However, for weak computers this might take forever.

BUILDING NEURAL NETWORK

Now that we have prepared our data, we can start building the neural network.

```
model = models.Sequential()
model.add(layers.Conv2D(32, (3, 3),
activation='relu',
                        input_shape=(32, 32, 3)))
model.add(layers.MaxPooling2D((2, 2)))
model.add(layers.Conv2D(64, (3, 3),
activation='relu'))
model.add(layers.MaxPooling2D((2, 2)))
model.add(layers.Conv2D(64, (3, 3),
activation='relu'))

model.add(layers.Flatten())
model.add(layers.Dense(64, activation='relu'))
model.add(layers.Dense(10, activation='softmax'))
```

Here we again define a *Sequential* model. Our inputs go directly into a convolutional layer (*Conv2D*). This layer has 32 filters or channels in the shape of 3x3 matrices. The activation function is the ReLU function, which we already know and the input shape is 32x32x3. This is because we our images have a resolution of 32x32 pixels and three layers because of the RGB colors. The result is then forwarded into a *MaxPooling2D* layer that simplifies the output. Then the simplified output is again forwarded into the next convolutional layer. After that into another max-pooling layer and into another convolutional layer. This result is then being flattened by the *Flatten* layer, which means that it is transformed into a one-dimensional vector format. Then we forward the results into one dense hidden layer before it finally comes to the softmax output layer. There we find the final classification probabilities.

TRAINING AND TESTING

Now we are almost done. We just need to train and test the model before we can use it.

```
model.compile(optimizer='adam',
loss='sparse_categorical_crossentropy',
            metrics=['accuracy'])
```

Here we again use the *adam* optimizer and the *sparse categorical crossentropy* loss function.

```
model.fit(train_images,
          train_labels,
          epochs=10,
          validation_data=(test_images,
test_labels))
```

We now train our model on our training data in ten epochs. Remember: This means that our model is going to see the same data ten times over and over again.

```
test_loss, test_acc = model.evaluate(test_images,
                                     test_labels,
                                     verbose=2)
```

We use the *evaluate* function to test our model and get the *loss* and *accuracy* values. We set the parameter *verbose* to 2, so that we get as much information as possible.

```
- 1s - loss: 0.8139 - acc: 0.7090
```

Your results are going to slightly differ but in this case I got an accuracy of around 70%. This is quite impressive when you keep in mind that we have ten possible classifications and the chance to be right by guessing is 10%. Also this task is way more complicated that classifying handwritten digits and we also have some similar image types like *car* and *truck* or *horse* and *deer*.

CLASSIFYING OWN IMAGES

However, the interesting part starts now. Since our model is trained, we can now go ahead and use our own images of cars, planes, horses etc. for classification. These are images that the neural network has never seen before. If you don't have your own images, you can use Google to find some.

Fig. 5.5: Car and horse

I chose these two pictures from Pixabay, since they are license-free.

The important thing is that we get these images down to 32x32 pixels because this is the required input format of our model. For this you can use any software like Gimp or Paint. You can either crop the images or scale them.

Fig. 5.6: Images in 32x32 pixels resolution

Now we just have to load these images into our script, using OpenCV.

```
img1 = cv.imread('car.jpg')
img1 = cv.cvtColor(img1, cv.COLOR_BGR2RGB)
img2 = cv.imread('horse.jpg')
img2 = cv.cvtColor(img2, cv.COLOR_BGR2RGB)
plt.imshow(img1, cmap=plt.cm.binary)
plt.show()
```

The function *imread* loads the image into our script. Then we use the *cvtColor* method, in order to change the default color scheme of BGR (blue, green, red) to RGB (red, green, blue).

```
plt.imshow(img1, cmap=plt.cm.binary)
plt.show()
```

With the *imshow* function, we can show the image in our script, using Matplotlib.

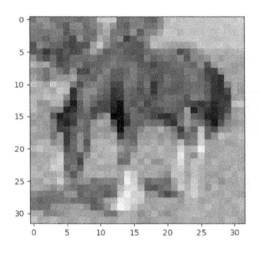

Fig. 5.7: Horse in Matplotlib

We can now use the loaded images as the input for our model, in order to get a prediction.

```
prediction = model.predict(np.array([img1]) /
255)
index = np.argmax(prediction)
print(class_names[index])
```

First we use the *predict* function to get the softmax result. Notice that we are converting our image into a NumPy array and dividing it by 255. This is because we need to normalize it, since our model was trained on normalized values. Then we use the *argmax* function to get the index of the highest softmax activation value. Finally, we print the class name of that index as a result.

```
Car Horse
```

The results speak for themselves. These pictures were classified absolutely correct. Of course this will not always be the case. Sometimes a deer will be classified as a horse and vice versa. But the performance of our model is still pretty impressive.

Again I encourage you to experiment and play around with that model. Try to change the parameters of the network. Try to classify other images. Maybe use completely different training data with different possible class names. Make sure that you feel comfortable using convolutional neural networks.

6 – REVIEW AND RESOURCES

We have learned quite a lot in these five chapters and some of the topics were quite complex. Thus we are going to quickly review all the concepts in this final chapter and add some additional information and resources.

REVIEW: BASICS

The first chapter was probably the most confusing one, since it was highly theoretical and mathematical. It is your choice how deep you want to go into that matter.

If you really want to become a machine learning expert, innovate and develop new technologies in this field, a solid understanding of the detailed mathematics is probably necessary.

However, if you are not interested in the details of machine learning theory and you just want to apply the technologies, this is not necessary. For example you won't need any higher mathematical skills for developing a basic fitness app which uses machine learning. You only need to know how to use Tensorflow and other libraries properly.

As soon as you go into research or innovation though, there is no way around math.

At this point check if you really understand the following concepts:

- Neural networks and their structure
- Structure of perceptrons
- Activation functions
- Training and testing models
- Error and loss
- Gradient descent algorithm
- Backpropagation

If there is anything that you feel you didn't quite understand, read through the first chapter one more time. Also learn to google and research problems and questions properly. Every programmer encounters a lot of errors, mistakes and confusions while coding. You cannot cover all of these in one book. Therefore, don't be afraid to use Google, StackOverflow, Documentations and YouTube. Professional developers do this as well.

REVIEW: NEURAL NETWORKS

In the third chapter we talked about the basics of Tensorflow. We built a first simple neural network and used it to classify handwritten digits. If you didn't understand something at this point, you probably also had some problems with the following chapters, since they build on this one. So make sure that you really master this chapter.

Ask yourself if you understand the following concepts:

- Loading datasets from Keras
- Splitting training and testing data

- Building neural networks with Tensorflow
- Compiling models
- Training and testing models in code
- Loading and preparing your own images

Also take some time to be creative and think about ways in which you could use all of that knowledge. What can you use neural networks for? What problem can you solve? What data could you predict? We did just one example in this chapter. Research some datasets and play around with them.

Keras Datasets: https://keras.io/datasets/

Scikit-Learn Datasets:
https://scikit-learn.org/stable/datasets/index.html

REVIEW: RECURRENT NEURAL NETWORKS

Here the topics got more interesting. We started using recurrent neural networks and thus adding a memory to our model. We used the model to generate poetic texts like those of Shakespeare.

A big part of the work in this chapter was preprocessing and preparing our data and also working with the output in a proper way.

The challenge wasn't really with building recurrent neural networks. It was pretty easy to add an LSTM layer. But converting our text into a numerical format, then transforming it into NumPy arrays, training the network, then again converting the output and generating text was a challenge. But you need to get used to that. Oftentimes the machine learning model is very easy to build. But when we need to work with real-world data instead of perfect datasets from Keras, things become harder. In the real world the data is chaotic and not at all preprocessed or prepared. So it is very crucial that you master this part as well.

Ask yourself if you understand the following concepts:

- Loading online data into the Python script
- Preprocessing and structuring data so that it can be further processed by neural networks
- Basic advantages of LSTM layers
- Workings of recurrent neural networks

Of course, here you should also experiment a little bit. Use different data. Everything that is sequential will work in some way. Maybe you want to use different texts or a different network structure. Maybe you want to predict weather data or stock prices. Be creative and work on your own mini-projects to master the skills.

REVIEW: CONVOLUTIONAL NEURAL NETWORKS

Last but not least we also used convolutional neural networks. These are especially useful when we need to recognize patterns like in images or audio files.

We used a Keras dataset with numerous pictures of ten different possible object types. Our neural network was able to classify these objects with an accuracy of 70%, which is pretty impressive.

Ask yourself if you understand the following concepts:

- Convolutional layers
- Pooling layers and pooling functions
- Filtering or channels and matrices

And once again: Experiment! Maybe create your own set of pictures and labels. Then use it as training data and build a model that classifies the people of your family or the different tools on your desk. Use other datasets and research how to use convolutional neural networks for audio processing. Maybe you can build a voice or speech recognition bot.

NEURALNINE

One place where you can get a ton of additional free resources is *NeuralNine*. This is my brand and it has not only books but also a website, a YouTube channel, a blog, an Instagram page and more. On YouTube you can find high quality video tutorials for free. If you prefer text, you might check out my blog for free information. The *neuralnine* Instagram page is more about infographics, updates and memes. Feel free to check these out!

YouTube: https://bit.ly/3a5KD2i

Website: https://www.neuralnine.com/

Instagram: https://www.instagram.com/neuralnine/

Can't wait to see you there! ☺

What's Next?

When you have understood the concepts in this book and are able to apply them, you have progressed in your programming career a lot. You have made a huge step. These skills are invaluable in today's world but even more so in the future.

You are able to digitalize data from the real world, process it, forward it into a neural network and then make predictions or decisions based on that. Some might argue that this is a little bit like magic.

Depending on the field of application that you are interested in, you will need to learn some additional skills. No book on earth can teach you everything. If you want to apply that knowledge in the finance field, you will need to learn about stocks, insurances etc. If you want to use it for medical or sports purposes, you will need to educate yourself on that. Computer science and mathematics alone will probably not get you very far, unless you go into research. However, it is the basis of everything and you should now have this basis. Whether you choose to predict the weather or build the next space exploration company is up to you.

If you are interested in finance programming however, check out my Amazon author page. There I have some additional books and one of them (volume five) is about finance programming in Python. Alternatively you can also find them on the NeuralNine website.

Books: https://www.neuralnine.com/books/

Last but not least, a little reminder. This book was written for you, so that you can get as much value as possible and learn to code effectively. If you find this book valuable or you think you learned something new, please write a quick review on Amazon. It is completely free and takes about one minute. But it helps me produce more high quality books, which you can benefit from.

Thank you!

NeuralNine

If you are interested in free educational content about programming and machine learning, check out https://www.neuralnine.com/

There we have free blog posts, videos and more for you! Also, you can follow the ***@neuralnine*** Instagram account for daily infographics and memes about programming and AI!

Website: https://www.neuralnine.com/

Instagram: @neuralnine

YouTube: NeuralNine